Rise Beyond Fears

Anthems of Positivity

Dr. Anupam Kurlwal (Acharya)

BookLeaf
Publishing

India | USA | UK

Made with ❤ on the BookLeaf Publishing Platform

www.bookleafpub.in

www.bookleafpub.com

Dedication

For the dreamers, the believers, the doers —
Who refuse to bow before their fears,
And dare to rise, again and again.
For those still finding the strength to stand —
This book is a hymn to your courage,
A melody to guide you through the storm.
To the fearless within the fearful —
May these anthems awaken your wings,
And remind you that rising is your habit.

Preface

Rise Beyond Fears – Anthems of Positivity
In a world that moves relentlessly, where challenges and uncertainties greet us at every turn, the human spirit often seeks guidance, courage, and hope. Rise Beyond Fears – Anthems of Positivity is a collection of 21 poems crafted to inspire resilience, ignite ambition, and illuminate the path to self-discovery. Each poem is a beacon, a motivational anthem, and a call to rise above limitations.

1. **Rise Through Hard Work** – A celebration of diligence, perseverance, and self-discipline, reminding us that effort defines our destiny.
2. **The Price of Greatness – A Poem of Responsibility** – Teaches accountability, wise decision-making, and the courage to lead with integrity.
3. **Rise Beyond Fears – Anthem of Positivity** – Encourages courage, patience, and unwavering commitment to personal growth.
4. **The Heart's True Song – A Chant of Values** – Emphasizes principles, moral strength, and the enduring power of integrity.
5. **The Poem of Purpose** – Explores life's higher calling, the importance of passion, and the transformative power of mission-driven living.

6. **The Wealth of Twenty-Four** – Celebrates time as the ultimate treasure, urging mindful living and purposeful use of each day.

7. **Keep Smiling** – Promotes joy, optimism, kindness, and the contagious power of a positive attitude.

8. **The Gift of Time and Words** – Reminds us of the preciousness of our words and actions, encouraging thoughtful, intentional living.

9. **The Mirror of Life** – Highlights self-reflection, growth through critique, and the cultivation of wisdom in daily life.

10. **The Cave and the Sun** – Inspires stepping beyond comfort zones to embrace growth, courage, and the vast possibilities of life.

11. **Vision: The Art of Seeing Beyond** – Guides the reader to look beyond the obvious, balance priorities, and live purposefully.

12. **The True Leader's Anthem** – Elevates the principles of noble leadership, selflessness, and uplifting others.

13. **Passionate Profession — The Sacred Calling** – Celebrates the sanctity of work, mastery, and dedication to one's craft.

14. **Friendship — A Bond Beyond Blood** – Captures the essence of authentic friendship, loyalty, and emotional connection.

15. **Money: The Powerful Companion** – Reflects on financial wisdom, responsible management, and the ethical use of resources.
16. **Parents and Teachers — Two Architects of a Child** – Honors the dual guiding forces shaping a child's life: love and education.
17. **The True Measure of Love** – Explores the balance of passion, wisdom, and practical responsibility in human relationships.
18. **Goal Mind: Success Begins Within** – Focuses on internal motivation, disciplined focus, and strategic goal setting.
19. **The Power of Belief** – Celebrates faith in oneself, perseverance, and the transformative strength of self-belief.
20. **Faith — The Fire Within** – Encourages trust, hope, and action guided by faith, showing that belief is a force beyond logic.
21. **The Seven Duties of Youth** – A motivational call to the youth, highlighting personal growth, social responsibility, and nation-building.

This collection is not merely a book of poems; it is a companion for the mind and soul. Each piece carries a unique strength—some ignite courage, some instill discipline, some nurture kindness, and others illuminate purpose. Together, they form a symphony of positivity, urging readers to rise beyond fears, embrace life's trials, and celebrate every victory, big or small.

Rise Beyond Fears – Anthems of Positivity is a journey through the valleys of doubt toward the summits of self-belief. Each verse awakens the quiet strength that resides within every heart, reminding us that courage is not the absence of fear, but the will to rise despite it.

In a world often clouded by uncertainty, these poems are rays of renewal—echoing faith, resilience, and the unbreakable human spirit. They are not written to preach, but to reach; not to instruct, but to inspire. Whether you stand at the crossroads of choice or at the dawn of new beginnings, may these lyrical anthems become your companion in rediscovering hope.

Every poem in this collection carries a pulse—of optimism, endurance, and transformation. They celebrate the power of belief, the beauty of gratitude, and the joy of simply rising again, stronger than before.

May *Rise Beyond Fears* remind you that no night is too dark, no storm too fierce, and no dream too distant—if you choose to believe, strive, and rise.

— *Dr. Anupam Kurlwal (Acharya)*

Acknowledgements

With a heart full of gratitude, I wish to thank those who have shaped this journey and inspired the words you now hold in your hands.

To my father, (Late) Sh. D. S. Kurlwal, whose life remains a source of strength and motivation. A true parent in every sense—your values, love, and guidance continue to inspire me.

To my mentor, Prof. (Dr.) Naresh Sharma, your guidance in honing my writing and nurturing original thought has been a light on my path. Your belief in my ideas gave me the courage to trust my own voice.

To Prof. (Dr.) Gurpal Singh, thank you for teaching me the power of discipline and dedication. Your lessons continue to remind me that perseverance is the key to transforming dreams into reality.

I am grateful to the hard times and challenges I have faced—though they tested me, they also fueled my creativity and gave life to these poems.

To all the wonderful souls who stood by me, believed in

me, and offered their support during difficult moments—
this book carries a piece of your encouragement in every
line.

And to Book Leaf, my publisher, thank you for believing
in this work and giving me the opportunity to share
these anthems of hope and positivity with the world.

This book is a celebration of mentors, moments of
struggle, and the unwavering support of those who
believed in me. From the depths of my heart, thank you

1. Rise Through Hard Work

Work hard each day, let your fire ignite,
Daily dedication fuels your inner light.
Seeds of progress in sweat are sown,
Your rise or your fall is yours alone.

Be eager to grow, be steady, be strong,
The process is hard but your heart holds on.
Knowledge is the key, courage leads the way,
Through skill and effort, you conquer the day.

Dreams are not gifts, they're goals to pursue,
Each trial you face carves a stronger you.
The climb may be steep, the journey feels long,
But dawn always breaks for the bold and strong.

Rise with resolve, let challenge be faced,
Progress is born when persistence is chased.
Each step you take, each effort you show,
Builds the success that helps you grow.

Stand tall through the storm, let faith be your shield,
No battle is lost when you refuse to yield.
Destiny bows to the brave and the true —
The power to rise has always been in you.

Through hard work you rise, through guidance you shine,
The future is yours, the victory divine.

2. The Price of Greatness – A Poem of Responsibility

Responsibility—the greatest liberty,
To choose each response with clarity.
To act, not react, with a leader's grace,
For slavery ends when action takes place.

The weaker self reacts, the wiser self leads,
Life is but a journey of chosen deeds.
The buck must stop where leaders stand,
Guiding others with a helping hand.

When all thought someone surely would,
None did the good that all could.
Blame is easy, yet truth sustains:
Your choices are yours—losses or gains.

Four wise monkeys teach us true:
See the good, speak true, hear with care, act through.
Pause before action, proceed with care,
Think through each choice, be aware.

Each morning plan your dos and don'ts,
Each night reflect on what worked, what won't.
Greatness is born when excuses die,
Awake, take charge, set your standards high!

Rise with purpose, let nothing restrain,
Seize your greatness, break every chain!

3. Rise Beyond Fears –
Anthem of Positivity

Prepare and perspire, train for your best game,
Discipline and dedication will carve out your name.
Do what's needed each day, let your to-do guide the way,
Mistakes are not to fear, they brighten your pathway.

Great dreams take time; they cannot be rushed through,
Step with care and vision, and watch them come true.
Face every challenge with courage in your heart,
Let focus and consistency never depart.

Hold on to courage when the road feels too long,
Each small win will make your spirit more strong.
Rise after each fall, with resolve that won't break,
Your journey is yours—be wise in each step you take.

Celebrate small wins, for they keep you the road,
Patience and persistence will lighten your load.
Hold vision and mission as shields on your quest,
With heart and hard work, you'll give out your best.

Ego must fade, let humility stay,
Like fruitful trees bending, strength on display.
Share what you learn, guide others along,
Shine as a beacon--wise, kind, and strong.

Rise beyond fears, let nothing hold you down,
Stand tall, be yourself, and claim your crown!

4. The Heart's True Song – A Chant of Values

Stand as a warrior but calm and still,
Observe your heart and honor your will.
Love yourself first, let respect begin,
Only then can true love flow within.

Gold stays gold, through scratches and time,
Worth does not fade, it rings like a chime.
Know yourself deeply, let wisdom arise,
Right thinking blooms in the choices you prize.

Claim your iron axe, leave silver and gold,
Honesty's treasure is richer than told.
Respect is earned; it cannot be forced,
Give it, receive it, let rule run its course.

Loyalty chooses; true friends are few,
Though critics rise, still stand tall and true.
Step by step, gain wisdom each day,
Let values guide you; let darkness give way.

Treat others as you wish to be treated,
Love freely, act justly, let life be completed.
Resonate softly, resonate strong,
A life of values—the heart's true song.
A life of values—the heart's true song.

Stand tall in truth, let your spirit roar,
Walk the path of light, shine ever more.
Let the heart's true song forever soar.

5. The Poem of Purpose

The purpose of life
is the search itself—
to seek the gift,
to heal, to uplift.
Great souls live
for a mission, for fire;
while common minds chase
what crowds admire.

If you are breathing,
your mission's not done.
Let passion be your compass,
God's will your sun.
Live and act
with ideals in mind,
lift souls with your God-given gift,
spread love that is kind.

Lead not by command,
but by helping all grow.

Make leaders of leaders,
let true greatness show.
In trial, ask softly:
"What would my ideal do?"
The whisper within
will guide you through.

When the last treat is given,
and your story is read,
may love be the echo
of the life you led.
Applause will vanish,
events will fade;
but purpose endures
in the lives we made.

Leave the sparks that turn darkness to dawn,
and carry the torch long after you're gone.

6. The Wealth of Twenty-Four

We all are given, none gets more,
A gift of time—just twenty-four.
Not gold, nor land, nor money rare,
But fleeting hours we each must care.

Complain, and still the clock will run,
The day will fade, the night be done.
Act with courage, learn, and try,
And watch your spirit soar and fly.

In youth, let failure be your guide,
With open heart and fearless stride.
In middle years, build what is true,
Let passion shape the work you do.

And later, teach, uplift, and show,
The seeds you plant will surely grow.
Then rest at last, be wisdom's store,
The legacy of twenty-four.

For time is life, and nothing less,
A chance to grow, to dream, to bless.
So guard each hour, and make it shine,
The wealth of twenty-four is mine.

Waste or invest, for none gets more,
Your crown of life is twenty-four.

7. Keep Smiling

Keep smiling--don't let it fade,
Joy in your heart is the choice you made.
With every step, let kindness guide,
Love will walk right by your side.

Never look sad; just wear a smile,
It makes the journey worth each mile.
Accept your flaws, let caring show,
Appreciate others and help them grow.

Follow your leader, stand side by side,
Forget the hurt, let peace reside.
Forgive the sinner, your soul will improve,
With love in your heart, keep life on the move.

Dream with courage, act with grace,
Leave your mark, your sacred trace.
Lift the fallen, ignite their flame,
In serving others—you rise to fame.

Meet and greet the souls you find,
Travel, dine, laugh--hearts aligned.
Spread your light and let it shine,
Build a better world, yours and mine.

Laugh often, love always--
Life is short, love more always.

8. The Gift of Time and Words

The truest guide, your dearest friend,
Is self-experience, till the end.
Through trials met and lessons earned,
Life's deepest truths are slowly learned.

Use your time as if pure gold,
Each fleeting moment, each tale told.
Speak with care, let words take flight,
For once released, they fade from sight.

No second chance, no borrowed day,
Time slips silently and drifts far away.
Words once spoken cannot return—
A lesson hard we all must learn.

So treasure both with mindful heart,
In every end, in every start.
Life is swift, yet honest and true;
What you give will come to you.

Live with schedule, think before you say,
Let vision and mission guide your way.
For in the end, when all is through,
The life well-lived reflects in you.

The path is yours, the choice is too,
Choose them well, for they shape you.

9. The Mirror of Life

If you wish for joy, let praises near,
But to grow in strength,welcome critique clear.
Look within,in quiet reflect,
And cleanse your soul of every defect.

Hands will join when triumphs gleam,
Yet few will walk along your dream.
No act is wholly good or wrong,
Each note composes life's own song.

A time will come, as all shall see,
When life unfolds,experience free.
Not loss,nor gain but wisdom's call—
A journey shared by one and all.

Speak with mind, yet listen well,
In every story, wisdom dwells.
The smallest act, the kindest word,
Can lift a soul that's rarely heard.

With softened heart and mind made wise,
Forgive the faults you recognize.
For peace is found not in the fray,
But in the grace you hold today.

So face the mirror, embrace it all;
Hold your reflection,and rise tall.

10. The Cave and the Sun

Within the cave, where shadows rest,
The mind feels safe, the heart feels blessed.
Familiar walls, a gentle chain--
A comfort wrapped in quiet pain.

But step beyond that guarded door,
And sunlight strikes--too bright, too raw.
It blinds, it burns, it makes you weep,
And tempts you back to darkness deep.

Yet if you stand, endure the glare,
The world unfolds, the colors flare.
Your sight returns, the truth is clear--
The cave was small, the sky is near.

Though growth begins with aching eyes,
It leads to vast, unending skies.
The pain will fade, the light will stay,
And guide you on your truest way.

So rise, brave soul, let fear release,
Embrace the vastness, embrace your peace.
For those who dare to leave the night,
Will walk in strength, and shine in light.

No cave can cage what's made to soar--
Step out, the world holds so much more.

11. Vision: The Art of Seeing Beyond
(Anthem of Vision)

Vision is the art divine,
To see the stars before they shine.
To glimpse the dawn through darkest night,
And walk by faith, not by sight.

Mission shows what, ethics shows how,
Vision reveals the where and now.
Half the journey's already drawn,
When you behold the destined dawn.

Success is not a goal to chase,
But a rhythm, a state--a steady grace.
It's not what you earn, but what you retain—
The joy of relevance beyond the gain.

In seven realms your life must grow—
Career, family, finance flow,

Friends, health, social, spirit's flame,
Balance them all—none the same.

Ask yourself, "Why am I here?"
Let your purpose be loud and clear.
At life's last breath, let truth proclaim —
Believe, achieve, leave your name.

Practice, plan, let your dreams arise,
For vision soars when mission flies.

12. The True Leader's Anthem

Listen close! Hear the call!
Selfishness blinds us all—
Blind to self, blind to truth, blind to humankind.
When greed and jealousy rise,
The heart grows small, the spirit dies!

To praise another—that's a brave ask !
It takes a valiant and fearless heart.
Those alike in strength and flame
Too often clash for power, not for aim.

Lead with grace! Do not cling!
Time will crown the next worthy king.
Forget the chains of blood and name,
Bestow honor where it's rightly claimed!

Envy, pride, position, fame—
All the same in the ruthless game.
But legends—true legends—never fade,

They shine through those they've led and made.

Stand tall! Speak truth! Lift every heart!
Leadership is more than a throne—it's a noble craft!
The world remembers not the crown you bore,
But the lives you lifted, forevermore!

A leader's glory is not control,
It's raising souls to take the role.

13. Passionate Profession —
The Sacred Calling

Work is worship when joy's your guide,
Success walks humbly by your side.
Be your truest self—no copy made,
Better a bold fall than a safe parade.

Enjoy the process, love the climb,
Each step a prayer, each hour sublime.
Unfold the gift that God has sown—
Your strength, your spark, uniquely your own.

Timetables fail, but focus wins,
Single-mindedness—the crown of kings.
Be like the cobra—calm, precise, and wise,
Not the octopus with scattered ties.

Don't train the heart—awaken your sense,
Let wonder be your evidence.
Peace, joy, and truth your spirit find,
Where soul and work are intertwined.

Choose commitment over comfort's call,
Perfect practice conquers all.
Opportunity waits beneath your shoe—
Do what you love, and love what you do.

Two days divine in life we see—
The day we're born, the day we be.

14. Friendship — A Bond Beyond Blood
(An Ode to True Friendship)

Friends are chosen, kin imposed by fate,
No caste, no creed can separate.
No colour, gender, or worldly test—
Just hearts that beat in mutual quest.

They're brothers, sisters—souls aligned,
A meeting of hearts, a mirror of mind.
When trials rise and troubles call,
True friends stand firm through it all.

A friend in need—so rare, so true,
While others preach, they stand by you;
With silent strength and helping hand,
They lift you up, they help you stand.

They never flatter, nor falsely cheer,
They speak the truth you need to hear.

By love or force, they make you see
The best within who you can be.

With friends, no mask, no need to hide,
You share your scars, your victories, pride.
A true friend's worth no gold can measure—
Hold them close—life's rarest treasure.

No force can break the bond friends share,
A friend's true love is beyond compare.

15. Money: The Powerful Companion
(Ode to Money)

Oh Money, humble yet profound,
Not god, not demon, but power unbound.
Like petrol in the car we drive,
You fuel our journey, keep dreams alive.

In coins and notes, you pass from hand to hand,
An exchange of value, a life well planned.
In wealth, you shine—a fortress, a gate,
In debt, you burden, dictate our fate.

Teach me, O Money, the art of your lore:
Earn while learning, invest evermore.
Save for the storms, spend with care,
Freedom lies not in riches rare.

Let simplicity be my chosen creed,
Live within means, for greed misleads.

Dresses, watches, fleeting delight,
Bank balances, properties—true wealth in sight.

Three pillars strong, you stand in form:
Savings, investments, insurance—protect from storm.
Misused, you bind; used wisely, you soar,
A key to freedom, power, and more.

Oh Money, neither master nor slave,
A tool, a servant, yet bold and brave.

16. Parents and Teachers — Two Architects of a Child (An Ode to Future Makers)

Parenting and teaching—two sides of a coin,
In shaping a child, their hearts combine.
At home sixteen hours, at school just eight,
Sixteen to nurture, eight to educate.

Parents lead not by words, but by deed,
Character blooms where love builds the creed.
A father—the first man a girl perceives,
A mother—the first woman a boy believes.

Teach through presence, correct with grace,
Not to command, but to guide in life's race.
A home gives roots, a school gives wings,
Two sacred spaces where growth begins.

Both must work with heart and vision,
To raise a wise, strong, noble citizen.

Independence—earned, by age and stage,
Wisdom nurtured, not trained in cage.

Values explained, not merely decreed,
Let curiosity and kindness lead.
When home and school in harmony align,
A triangle sacred—pure, divine.

A child's mind—a garden, tender and wide,
Needs the love of parents, and teachers as guide.

17. The True Measure of Love

Love at first sight still sparks a fire,
A heart that races, full of desire.
It seeks your time, your thoughts, your gaze,
Day and night lost in passion's maze.

We share our dreams, our laughs, our tears,
Moments that feel beyond the years.
Gifts and gestures, closeness, care,
A world too sweet for any to share.

But time will turn the thrill to routine,
Long talks fade, outings grow lean.
"I love you" spoken, hollow, bare,
Words without feeling float in the air.

Love is deep, yet must be wise,
A balance seen through careful eyes.
Blend it with work, with money, with health,
Family, friends—life's truest wealth.

Feel with your heart, but keep in your mind,
Let love uplift, not make you blind.
Emotions strong, yet purpose clear,
This is love—the kind we need dear.

Through storms and trials, love endures,
A guiding support, forever sure.

18. Goal Mind: Success begins within

Not talent, but focus; not luck, but aim,
The average man can win the game.
You get what you set—so set it right,
Dream in your mind, then act day and night.

Dogs chase cars, yet gain no prize,
Empty pursuits deceive the wise.
A failed success still stands tall—
Better that, than no try at all.

Skip the leaves, the branches high,
And fix your gaze on the bird's eye.
Aim for the moon—let vision ignite,
If you miss the stars, God bless your flight.

For success begins not when you start,
But when you believe—with mind and heart.
Set goals SMART—clear, real, and timed,
Half achieved once well-defined.

Choose what's yours—peace or possession?
Heartfelt living, or mere succession?
Seek accuracy, not blind precision—
One true strike fulfills the mission.

Every step—a goal complete,
Each inch forward—success concrete.

19. The Power of Belief
(A Motivational Lyric)

Conceive, believe, and you'll achieve,
The secret lies in what you believe.
No crown of gold, no royal crest—
Yet faith in self outshines the rest.

A real hero does what he can,
He stands alone, yet shapes the clan.
So take your pen, and write your creed,
Plant strong beliefs—uproot the weed.

Success begins where discipline starts,
From diaries, dreams, and daring hearts.
From prayers that calm, from hope that steers,
From battles won o'er inner fears.

"I can" outweighs the highest IQ,
Disbelief may touch the best of you—
But faith still beats within their chest,
For hearts that trust are truly blessed.

Winners don't wait for fate's direction,
They carve their path through self-perfection.
Think one great thought—live, breathe, and be,
Let no distraction capture thee.

For friend or foe, it's only me
Who writes my own biography.

20. Faith — The Fire Within

Belief is a spark, but faith is a flame,
Belief wins a race, faith rewrites the game.
Belief says "try," but faith says "done,"
Belief walks steady—faith begins to run.

Belief is logic, the mind's own art,
Faith isn't seeing—it's knowing by heart.
Find faith in the smallest—a smile, a seed,
Put creed in your action, in thought, and deed.

Think good, do good, feel good, stay true,
Whatever you send will return to you.
For God may not do what we ask or plan,
But He does what's right for every man.

Desire just dreams, hope takes the run,
Belief takes one step—faith wins the run.
When belief matures and stands the test,
Faith is your belief at its best.

The world belongs to hearts that try,
For faith is the power that touches the sky.
What can go right will go right,
Faith turns darkness into light.

Think, work, and expect the best—
With faith in your heart, you'll do the rest!

21. The Seven Duties of Youth

O youth of today, rise and shine,
The dawn of tomorrow is thine.
The nation awaits your noble deed,
Begin with self — in thought and creed.

First, worship the temple that's you,
Your body and mind — both sacred, true.
One hour to build, one hour to pray,
In sweat and silence, begin your day.

Second, wear grace, let confidence bloom,
Dress with purpose, drive out gloom.
Third, build your mind — your sharpest shield,
Through books and truth, let wisdom yield.

Fourth, lead not by noise, but voice refined,
To lift, enlighten, and guide mankind.
Fifth, seek your gift — your inner art,
Earn through skill yet give from heart.

Sixth, choose good friends — a priceless gain,
In joy and sorrow, share and sustain.
Seventh, build a home, a legacy wide,
Raise children strong, with dreams as guide.

O youth! The nation's hope is you —
Be pure, be wise, be bold, be true.

www.ingramcontent.com/pod-product-compliance
Lightning Source LLC
Chambersburg PA
CBHW070459050426
42449CB00012B/3052